how to think

50

PUZZLES

for

VISUAL
THINKING

how to think

50

PUZZLES
for
VISUAL
THINKING

CHARLES PHILLIPS

CONNECTIONS
BOOK PUBLISHING

For Melanie, Jim, and Tom

A CONNECTIONS EDITION
This edition published in Great Britain in 2009 by
Connections Book Publishing Limited
St Chad's House, 148 King's Cross Road, London WC1X 9DH
www.connections-publishing.com

Text and puzzles copyright © Bibelot Limited 2009
This edition copyright © Eddison Sadd Editions 2009

The right of Charles Phillips to be identified as the author of the work
has been asserted by him in accordance with the Copyright, Designs and
Patents Act 1988.

British Library Cataloguing-in-Publication data available on request.

ISBN 978-1-85906-306-4

1 3 5 7 9 10 8 6 4 2

Phototypeset in Bliss using QuarkXPress on Apple Macintosh
Printed in Singapore

CONTENTS

How to Think Visually

We live in a visual age. Images on the TV, the Internet, and in print leap across cultures; advertisements, web pages, magazine layouts, and movie shots are expertly designed to appeal to our visual sense.

As a result, it's more crucial than ever before to develop the capacity to think visually. People are "visually literate"—used to seeing well-designed pages and striking images. To appeal to others, whether we're making a presentation at work, developing a business idea, or laying out an essay, we need to know the basics of good visual presentation.

THE POWER OF PICTURES Pictures are simple, and have an immediate impact. An image can express a complex idea succinctly and inspirationally. Visual-thinking guru Dan Roam argues in his book *The Back of the Napkin* that in business meetings it's often more effective to present information or summarize discussions using simple pictures rather than graphs and bullet points. It can often be better to come up with these pictures "off the cuff" in the course of a meeting rather than to go in with meticulously planned presentations.

You may think, "But I can't draw" or "I probably have a poor visual sense." Don't be put off. Images of stick figures, arrows, boxes, and circles work just fine. According to Roam, the simpler the picture the more effective it is—and people who initially declare that they can't draw often come up with the most useful images.

WE CAN ALL THINK VISUALLY We are all born with great visual intelligence: consider, for example, the lavish imagery of our nightmares or daydreams. And most of us enjoyed drawing, painting, or modeling in our preschool years. Unfortunately, though, many of us find that over the years our natural capacity to think visually falls away—not least because educators tend to focus on numbers and words. But we can all revitalize our visual sense—you don't need to be a naturally gifted artist.

DAY-TO-DAY VISUAL THINKING There are many opportunities to practice thinking visually each day. Close your eyes and make an effort to visualize, say, the floorplan of your living room or the design of your ideal home. Imagine you have to hit the road; how would you go about packing your belongings into the trunk of your car?

If you're thinking about a problem, close your eyes to summon images and schematic representations of ideas. If you're trying to summarize information or present a plan to a colleague, try sketching it out.

THE BRAIN AND VISUAL THINKING Around half of your brain is engaged in the function of seeing. Visual information taken in by the eyes is processed in the occipital (or visual) cortex in the rear of the brain, then passed on to several other brain regions for analysis.

Many of the same brain regions used for processing what we see around us are used in recalling things we have seen and in imagining the future. One key role for your visual capacity is to visualize. You may use visualization to focus, calm yourself, or induce creativity, or you may want to visualize a better place for yourself in a year's time.

BOOST YOUR PERFORMANCE Developing your visual-thinking skills will improve your communication and may well help you land a job or improve your prospects at work; visual-thinking challenges are commonly used in psychometric employment tests and in assessment packages. In addition, getting to grips with visual thinking can be a wonderful time-saver—in all areas of your life.

The puzzles and challenges in this book will develop your ability to visualize complex shapes and patterns. By learning to translate ideas into images, you can put the power of visual thinking to work every day.

7

THE PUZZLES IN THIS BOOK There are three levels of puzzles to work through, each with a "time to beat" deadline. These deadlines apply a little pressure—we often think better when we set ourselves goals such as time constraints. But don't worry about these limits—they are no more than guidelines. So if you find that you are taking longer than the "ideal" time, relax. Look out for puzzles marked Time Plus. You'll almost certainly need a bit longer to complete these—not because they are more difficult, but because there's more work to do to solve them.

Some puzzles have another similar version later in the book, to give you even more practice. Where we feel you might need some help, a tip has been provided, and there are Notes and Scribbles pages at the back of the book to jot down your thoughts. Also toward the end of the book, the Challenge is designed to give your newly acquired visual-thinking skills a thorough work-out. This has a suggested time limit of 10–15 minutes to give you a chance to consider and reconsider the series of problems, to look for connections, visualize a solution, and perhaps make a few simple drawings in the margin space provided.

As your new skills develop, you'll find that you quickly see the effect in other areas of your life—by being able to see detail, spot patterns, and present ideas appealingly and succinctly. The benefits are many. So, look around, begin to "think visual," and let's get started!

PUZZLE GRADING	TIME TO BEAT
EASY = WARM-UP	1–2 MINUTES
MEDIUM = WORK-OUT	3–4 MINUTES
DIFFICULT = WORK HARDER	5–6 MINUTES
TIME-PLUS PUZZLES	6+ MINUTES
THE CHALLENGE	10–15 MINUTES

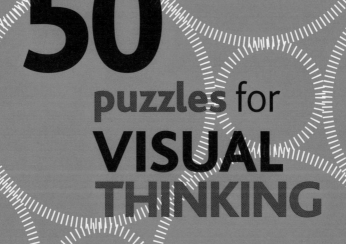

50 puzzles for VISUAL THINKING

Remember
Look **carefully**
Watch out for **details**
But don't miss **the bigger picture**
See **connections, patterns,**
and **analogies**
as you think **VISUALLY**

EASY
puzzles for
VISUAL
THINKING

The puzzles and thinking challenges in this
first section of the book give your visual-thinking
skills a warm-up. They're designed to provide
practice in seeing connections and visualizing
shapes, spatial relationships, and
effective analogies.

SUDOKU BAKE

Physics student Isaac works part-time in his uncle Sol's bakery. He designs a sudoku cake using chocolate math symbols for an end-of-year party, but then he has to rush away before he can finish the design and asks Uncle Sol to complete it, following some set rules. Can you help Sol fill up the grid?

The rules are simple: Every row, column, and 9 x 9 square must contain nine different chocolate symbols.

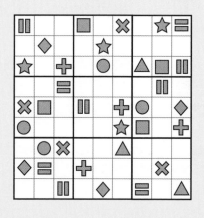

The four symbols missing from the top row are triangle, circle, cross, and diamond; by elimination you can work out that the second symbol from the left in the top row must be a triangle.

INK SPOT MUDDLE

Mr. Keitel, proprietor of stationery store The Ink Spot, took a short holiday and allowed his rather disorganized nephew Hans to look after the store. Now the stamp pads and their sample prints have become muddled. Can you help Mr. Keitel match stamp to print so he can show them to his client, Professor Potok?

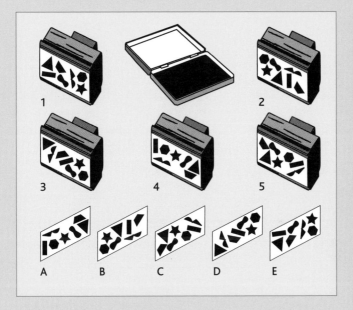

You can identify the print that matches stamp 4 by looking for a vertical bar on one side of the print.

PUZZLE 3 WARM-UP

TAI'S KEYRING CHALLENGE

In his job at the Garden Hotel, Tai often has to find a particular key quickly. He sets himself this challenge to speed up his recognition of different key shapes. Can you help him pair up these door keys with the impressions of their ends?

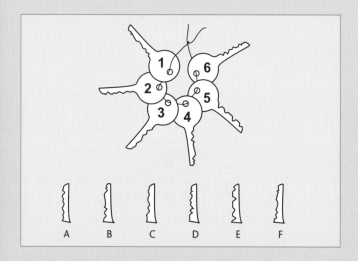

You'll speed up your response if you draw lines linking matching designs as you identify them.

FUTUREWORLD

Akinremi finds this challenge on Level 1 of his video game, FutureWorld. In the game, the world is icebound, and he has to judge how many cube-shaped blocks of ice are needed to fill the empty space so he can cross a canyon to reach the City of Gold. Can you help him?

Assume that all the blocks that cannot be seen from this angle are present. The overall design originally measured four blocks high, deep, and wide.

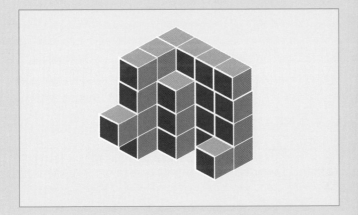

Try counting the missing blocks on each of the four layers.

CODE SYMBOL

Sunil devises this odd-one-out puzzle as a warm-up for the students on his mathematics course, Code Simple. He tells the students, "Each of these grid rectangles should contain no more and no less than one or more symbols from the numbered rectangle at the far left of its particular horizontal row, plus one or more symbols from the lettered rectangle at the top of its particular vertical column. However, one square doesn't follow this simple rule. Which is the odd one out?"

	A	B	C	D	E	F	G
	6 ♫	₪ 7	• 8	▼ }	% #	? +	$ ♦
1 £ 3	♫ 3	₪ 3	£ •3	▼ }£	% #3	+ 3	£ 3♦
2 ◄ X	6 X	X ₪	◄ •	◄ X▼	# X%	+ X?	$ ♦X
3 ♥ 0	6 0♫	₪ 0	8 0	♥ }	% 0#	+ ?	0 $
4 ♣ 4	4 6	7 4	• 4	♣ }	♣ %4	? 4	♣ ♦
5 5 ►	♫ ►6	₪ ►7	5 8	▼ ►}	► 5#	? +►	$ ►♦

how to **think** TIP

Sunil advises his students to check off one square at a time.

FORWARD AND BACK

Can you find your way from the entrance at top-left through the maze to the exit at bottom-right, passing through black dots only, then come back passing through gray dots only?

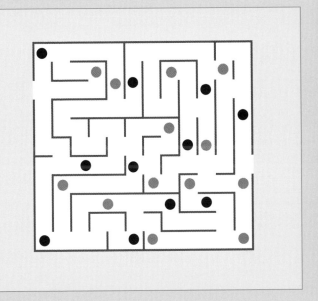

 how to think TIP

When traveling forward, you're looking for a route that avoids gray dots altogether. The route along the bottom of the design initially looks promising, but leads repeatedly into gray dots.

DANIELLE'S DESIGNS

Artist Danielle decorates teapots in variegated glazes for her aunt Katie's shop, Pour! Two of her six designs are identical, and Katie needs to find them quickly because a client, Brandon Brews, has asked for five teapots that are guaranteed to be unique. Can you help Katie spot the matching pair?

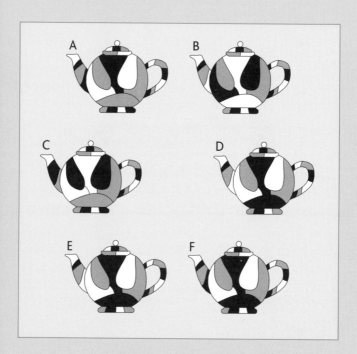

Look for identical spouts.

COUNTRYWIDE

Bennie is playing a video game called Countrywide, in which players build a life in the country, initially by taking over and running a farm. One task is a scarecrow-based spot the difference.

Every scarecrow differs in one way from the others. Can you help Bennie spot the one variation in every case?

Look at the crow as well as the scarecrow.

19

BUCKINGHAM'S BATTLESHIPS

Retired seadog Captain Buckingham devised this Battleships game for his friend and neighbor Jeremiah Gibson. The numbers on the side and bottom of the grid indicate occupied squares or groups of consecutive occupied squares in each row or column. Can you help Jeremiah fill up the grid so that it contains three cruisers, three launches, and three buoys, and the numbers make sense?

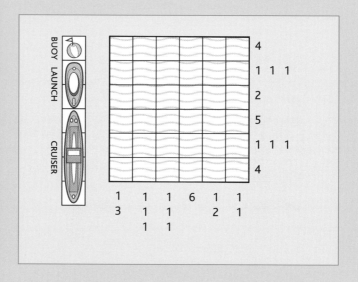

how to think TIP

The Captain says, "If I tell you there are no buoys in the top row that gets you on your way, Jeremiah, old chap."

BAZ TILES

Games designer Baz embeds this challenge into Look Here!, the visual-intelligence game he is developing for handheld game consoles. The challenge is to work out the pattern of the matrix and determine which of the boxed tiles (right) should fill the gap at bottom right.

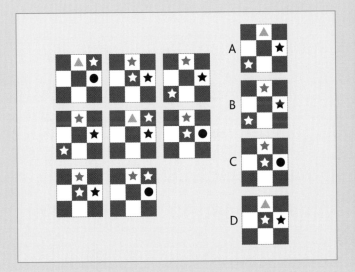

Look for patterns along rows and down columns.

LADY HARRIET'S HAT

Lady Harriet Walsingham wants a new hat, so visits her favorite milliner, Alfredo. She is difficult to please and tries on every hat in turn before randomly replacing them. Here are pictures of the display before and after Lady Harriet's visit. Which hat did she buy?

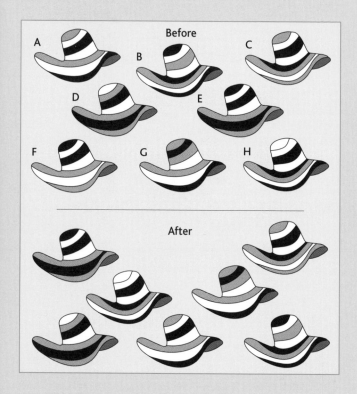

how to think TIP

As you work your way through the task, note down the letters of the hat designs you find present in the lower display.

MR. VERITY'S TANGRAMS

In the art department of the Upward Bounds High School, teacher Mr. Verity sets his students this tangram test. He asks them to re-create the shapes shown below using the seven tangram pieces shown (right).

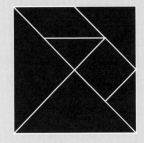

He tells them, "Remember, in each case you must use all of the pieces of the original tangram and they may not overlap."

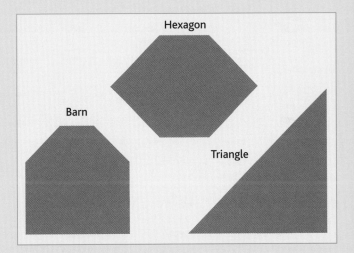

Hexagon

Barn

Triangle

how to think TIP

Get started by forming the roof of the barn. Its central section looks like it's a square.

23

DRESSMAKERS' CHALLENGE

Madame LeBrun asks the students at her dressmaking academy to reassemble four of the pieces of material shown to form the vase shape. They have to use two black and two white pieces. The pieces may be rotated, but not flipped over.

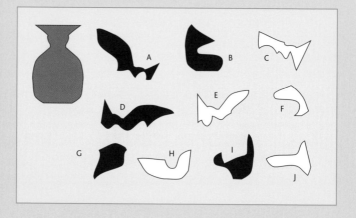

Try turning piece A counterclockwise.

ANCIENT TABLETS

Homer devises this code puzzle to put on a handmade 60th birthday card for his father, Armand, an anthropology professor and amateur archeologist. The question on the card reads: Which of the four alternatives (A, B, C, or D) should take the place of the question mark to continue the sequence of tablets?

how to think TIP

Rather than trying to see the progression of the whole block of nine squares, concentrate on one square at a time.

ANGEL'S JEWELS

Angel has a drawer full of jewels and decorations for mounting on rings. With little notice, she is asked to provide a collection for display at the Museum of Decorative Arts. Can you help her identify the only shape to appear twice?

Watch out for shapes that overlap others—and remember that the matching shapes you're looking for may be rotated.

ELVIS'S TIGHT FIT

Elvis creates this puzzle for his mother Rose, a retired teacher. He tells her, "Look at the four L-shapes shown outside the grid. A total of 12 L-shapes (three of each type) are inserted into the grid. Can you tell where the Ls are?"

He adds, "Each L-piece has a hole in it. Any piece may be turned or flipped over before being put in the grid. No pieces of the same kind may touch, even at a corner. The pieces fit together so well that you cannot see any spaces between them; only the holes show."

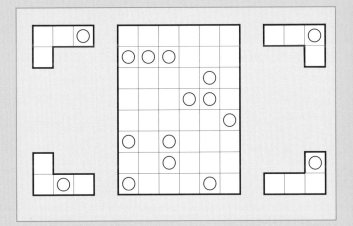

how to think TIP

Three holes together at the top-left of the design could be a good place to start.

27

MEDIUM
puzzles for
VISUAL
THINKING

The second section of the book contains medium-difficulty puzzles designed to give your visual-thinking skills a more demanding work-out. These puzzles provide training in seeing perspectives and patterns, while helping you develop your eye for detail, your short-term visual memory, and your powers of concentration.

PUZZLE 17 WORK-OUT

COUNTRYWIDE 2

Bennie encounters this spot-the-same challenge on Level 2 of his video game, Countrywide (see Puzzle 8). The player arrives in a wind-blown country field where six elves are flying kites. Only two of the kites are identical, and the task is to identify the matching pair within four minutes.

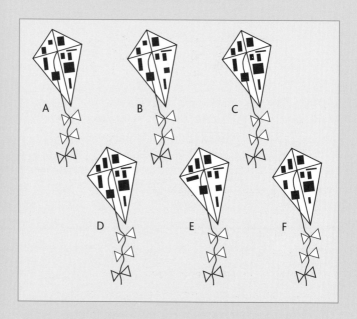

The top-right segment of the design is the same in all six kites, so you can ignore that.

TAI'S KEYRING CHALLENGE 2

At the Garden Hotel, Tai is promoted to night manager and he sets his new staff Tanika and Tan-yi a version of his key challenge (see Puzzle 3). They have to pair up these door keys with the impressions of their ends below. Can you help Tanika and Tan-yi?

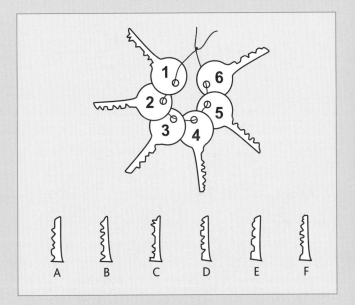

Start with keys 6 or 1—these are aligned almost vertically and can be compared more easily with their impressions below.

31

CHANCER'S SHADOW

Neville Chaunce, marketing manager at Gogglemoor Racetrack, devised this game as a promotion for the new Gogglemoor Great Flat Race. The test is to determine which of five shadows is that of Chancer, the bushy-tailed rearing horse shown here. The winner gets free entry to the race meeting.

Look at Chancer's tail as well as his legs.

ANCIENT TABLETS 2

Homer devises a second challenge for his father, Armand (see Puzzle 14). Here the tiles in the sequence contain the letters of the alphabet. As before, the challenge is to work out which of the four alternatives (A, B, C, or D) should take the place of the question mark, to complete the sequence.

M	Z	S
G	H	C
P	Z	V

I	V	O
J	K	F
N	X	T

E	R	K
M	N	I
L	V	R

?

A	N	G
O	Q	L
J	T	P

A

N	G	A
P	Q	L
J	S	P

B

A	N	G
P	Q	L
J	T	P

C

B	N	G
O	Q	L
J	T	P

D

how to think TIP

Bring your code-breaking skills to the table. Seek out the pattern in the letters.

MR. VERITY'S TANGRAMS 2

Here are some more of the tangram challenges devised by Mr. Verity of the Upward Bounds High School art department (see Puzzle 12). As before, try to create the shapes shown below using the seven tangram pieces provided (right). Remember, in each case you must use all of the pieces of the original tangram and they may not overlap.

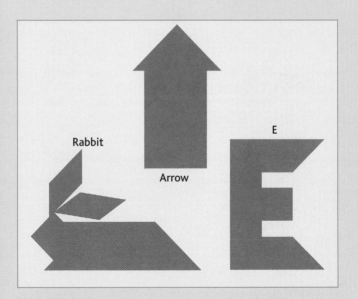

Rabbit

Arrow

E

There's only one piece that can be used to make the rabbit's lower ear.

34

INK SPOT MUDDLE 2

Mr. Keitel had to visit his mother in hospital and so asked Hans to look after his store, The Ink Spot (see Puzzle 2). Once again, Hans has allowed the stamps and sample prints to become muddled. Professor Potok is returning to view some new prints in a few minutes. Can you help Mr Keitel pair each stamp with its correct print?

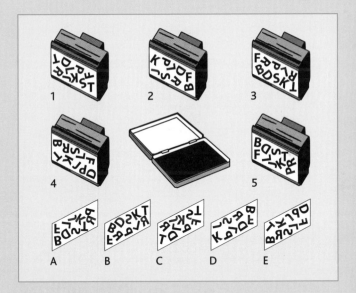

Why not draw a line between print and stamp when you identify a matching pair?

EJ'S CARPET CUBE

Furniture designer EJ comes up with this poser as a birthday present for his puzzle-mad friend Omar. He draws the designs below on card and asks Omar, "When the design is folded to form a cube, which of the cubes A–E would be produced?"

Can you help Omar? If Omar gets the answer right, EJ promises to make the design as a piece of furniture—a length of thick carpet that folds into a cube chair.

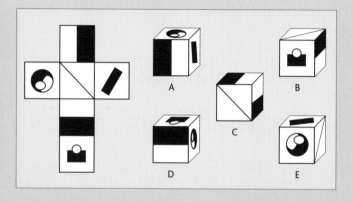

how to think TIP

If you first consider which faces could and could not be adjacent when the design is folded, certain answers are ruled out.

MASTER WILFRED WALSINGHAM'S SPINNING TOP

After Lady Walsingham has finished with her milliner, Alfredo (see Puzzle 11), she takes her son Master Wilfred to his favorite toy store, Jones Bros., to buy a new spinning top. Like his mother, Master Wilfred is hard to please and he handles each of the available tops in turn before randomly replacing them after he has made his choice. Here are pictures of the display before and after Master Wilfred's visit. Which spinning top does he buy?

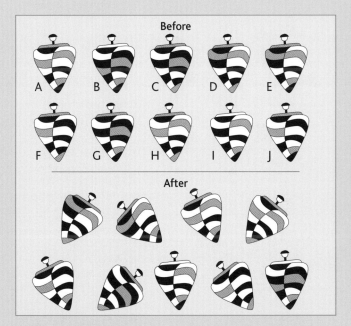

Before

A B C D E

F G H I J

After

how to think TIP Proceed logically. As before, you'll be able to master the challenge more easily if you tick off the letters of the spinning tops from the Before display as you find them in the After display.

ANGEL'S JEWELS 2

The display of Angel's jewelry at the Museum of Decorative Arts is going well (see Puzzle 15), and the curator asks for one more matching pair of jewels. Angel knows that she has one pair in her remaining jewelry tray. Can you help her find the only shape to appear twice? She is in a fluster because the courier has arrived early and is waiting!

Remember that for the purposes of the puzzle, when two or more shapes overlap we treat them as separate items rather than as one combined shape.

COUNTRYWIDE 3

Bennie has reached Level 3 of his video game, Countrywide (see Puzzles 8 and 17). This level is set in a sunny meadow on a summer's day. The player encounters five giant butterflies, and is told that each butterfly differs in one way from the others. Can you help Bennie spot the one difference in every case?

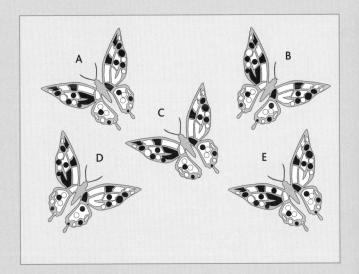

Butterfly B has a pretty obvious omission and makes an easy start.

HEX IN THE HOLE

Can you fit these seven hexagons into the central grid so that where one hexagon touches another along a bold line the contents of the adjacent triangles are the same? No rotation of any hexagon is allowed.

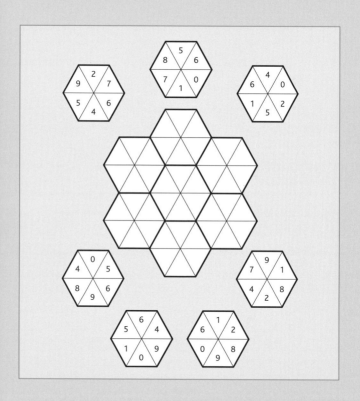

By elimination you should be able to narrow the options for the central hexagon.

FUTUREWORLD 2

Akinremi finds another missing-blocks challenge on Level 2 of his game, FutureWorld (see Puzzle 4). Level 2 of the game takes a mystical–religious turn: On windblown steppes, the player has to build up blocks of crystal in the shape of a perfect cube.

Can you help Akinremi? Assuming all the blocks that cannot be seen from this angle are present, how many blocks have been removed from this cube, which originally measured five blocks high, deep, and wide?

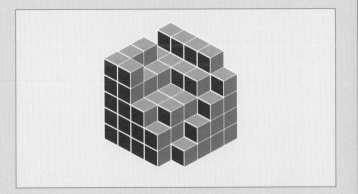

If you're counting the missing blocks one layer at a time, as before, build up from the bottom layer, where just one block is missing.

I HEART MATH

Art teacher Norton Park hangs a banner with the title "I Heart Math" in his studio. And each week he gets the students in his life class to do the sums in what he calls his "Symbol Challenge" at the start of their session.

Each symbol stands for a different whole number, none being less than one. In order to reach the correct total at the end of each line, what is the value of every symbol? Can you help Norton's students?

$$\frac{\square}{3} + \stackrel{\star}{} = 15$$

$$\stackrel{\star}{} - \triangle = \frac{\square}{4}$$

$$\frac{\triangle}{4} + \stackrel{\star}{} = \heartsuit$$

how to think TIP

Start by working out a value for the square, which is divisible by both 3 and 4, to make a whole number.

CHRISTINA'S CHOCOLATE CHALLENGE

Toward the end of a party, Christina arranged the remaining chocolates on a tray and issued this challenge to her friend and fellow philosophy student Angie: "Using just three straight lines, can you divide the arrangement into five sections, each of which contains six different types of chocolate?"

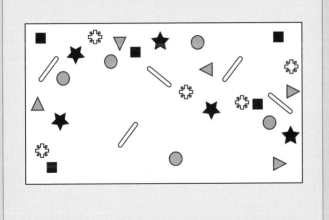

 It's fairly easy to isolate one set of six chocolate shapes in the top-left corner.

CLOCK CODE

Svetlana the spy receives the following instructions from her superior Dmitry: "Each day for four days, the clock in the town square will be stopped at an incorrect time. Work out the sequence, and determine what time should appear on the fifth day. Once you have the time, make contact in the usual way."

Count the minutes.

CODE SYMBOL 2

Sunil's students found they enjoyed his Code Symbol challenge (see Puzzle 5) and when one of them discovered the date of Sunil's 50th birthday, they devised their own version of the puzzle and printed it on a card. As before, each of the grid rectangles should contain no more and no less than one or more symbols from the numbered rectangle to the far left of its particular horizontal row, plus one or more symbols from the lettered rectangle at the top of its particular vertical column. However, one grid rectangle doesn't follow this rule, and the challenge is to determine which is the odd one out.

	A	B	C	D	E	F	G
	🔔 ☄	✷ 📖	♓ ○	♋ ♐	⚑ ●	☯ ✈	☯ ⧗
1	♇ ❄	♇ ☄	♇ 📖	○ ✷	❀ ♐	● ❀	☯ ♇	⧗ ❀ ♇
2	⬧ ♌	♌ ♎	📖 ✷ ⬧	♌ ○ ⬧	⬧ ♐ ♐	⬧ ♇ ♌	⬧ ✈	⬧ ☯
3	✋ ❀	✋ ☄	📖 ✷ ✋	❀ ○ ♓	✋ ♐ ❀	● ⚑ ❀	✈ ❀ ☯	✋ ☯
4	⬧ ⌸	⬧ ☄	✷ ⬧	❀ ○ ⌸	♋ ♐ ⌸	⚑ ⌸	⌸ ✈ ⬧	⧗ ⬧ ⌸
5	⬗ ♦	☄ ⬗ ♦ ♔	📖 ♦ ✷	⬗ ♓	♦ ♐ ⬗	● ⚑ ⬗	☯ ♦	⬗ ☯

how to think TIP

It may help to mark off symbols lightly in pencil as you find them.

DRESSMAKERS' CHALLENGE 2

Back at Madame LeBrun's dressmaking academy (see Puzzle 13), the top students are given this assembly challenge in their final exams. The challenge asks: "All but one of these pieces can be fitted together to form the camel shown. Which one is not required?"

The rules are very simple: The pieces may be rotated, but must not be flipped over.

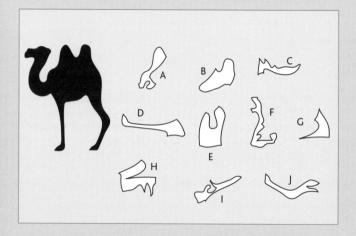

Two of the pieces will form the creature's distinctive legs.

ANDERS' LETTER GRID

Psychologist and expert puzzler Anders devises this letter-grid challenge for his colleague Ulla and leaves it on her desk. The challenge is to fit the letters A, B, C, D, E, and F into the grid in such a way that each horizontal row, each vertical column, and each of the heavily outlined sections of six squares contains the six letters. Some letters are already in place.

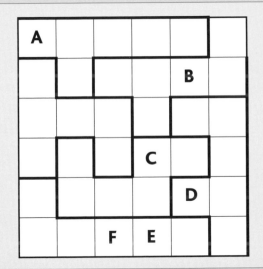

The L-shape in the bottom left may be the most promising place to start.

47

DIFFICULT
puzzles for
VISUAL
THINKING

You'll have to work harder to solve the puzzles in this
third part of the book, which contains the most
demanding of our exercises in visual thinking.
The puzzles further develop your powers of
visualization, as well as providing more practice in
working fast at a high level of detail. Before
attempting them, you may want to try a visual
warm-up: Move your eyes rapidly from left to right,
to the extremes of your peripheral vision; then, raise
a forefinger and alternate focus between your
fingertip and the most distant object you can see.

BUCKINGHAM'S BATTLESHIPS 2

Captain Buckingham, the retired seadog and Battleships aficionado (see Puzzle 9), has created a second layout of the same game for his neighbor, Jeremiah Gibson. As before, the numbers on the side and bottom of the grid indicate occupied squares or groups of consecutive occupied squares in each row or column.

Can you help Jeremiah fill up the grid so that it contains four cruisers, four launches, and four buoys, in such a way that the numbers make sense?

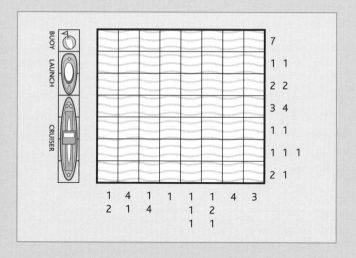

The captain says, "If I tell you that there are no buoys in the second row, that gives you an important clue about the alignment of the other vessels, old chap."

ELVIS'S TIGHT FIT 2

Puzzle-mad Elvis creates a second version of the Tight Fit puzzle he made for his mother, Rose (see Puzzle 16). This time he gives it to his friend Ella. He tells her, "Look at the four L-shapes shown outside the grid. A total of 12 L-shapes (three of each type) are inserted into the grid. Can you tell where the Ls are?"

He adds, "Each L-piece has a hole in it. Any piece may be turned or flipped over before being put in the grid. No pieces of the same kind may touch, even at a corner. The pieces fit together so well that you cannot see any spaces between them; only the holes show."

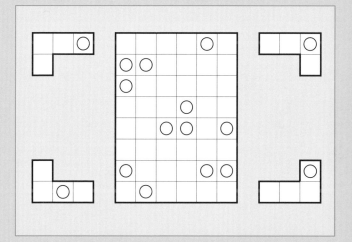

As before, a concentration of three holes together—at the top-left or in the center of the design—provides a good place to start.

THE SKELETON OF SØREN SØRENSEN

Karen, the wife of marketing manager Neville Chaunce (see Puzzle 19), borrows the shadow idea from her husband for a promotion at the Castle Museum in which she works. The museum website shows one of its prize exhibits—the skeleton of famous Danish explorer Søren Sørensen and four possible shadows. The task is to determine which shadow is that of Søren Sørenson's skeleton.

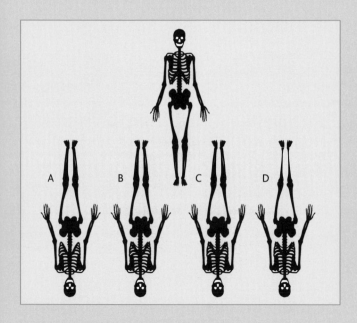

Start with the hands.

FUTUREWORLD 3

A third missing-blocks challenge is the opening puzzle on Level 3 of Akinremi's video game, FutureWorld (see Puzzles 4 and 28). At this level, the player is at the top of a sheer mountain seeking a way to meet a meditating guru. Can you help Akinremi judge how many cube-shaped rocks of incense are needed to build a perfect six-layer cube on which the player must meditate prior to climbing toward the guru's cave?

As before, assume that all the blocks that cannot be seen from this angle are present. How many blocks have been removed from the large cube, which originally measured six blocks high, deep, and wide?

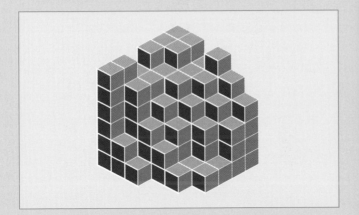

Try a different approach by working out the total number of blocks in a 6 x 6 layer and subtracting missing blocks from this total for each layer.

NO WAY OUT?

There seems to be no way out of this maze. But if you can find a path from one dot to the other, you activate a secret trapdoor beneath the second dot.

Starting at the upper dot, head up, then left.

SUDOKU BAKE 2

Isaac's chocolate symbol cake is a hit (see Puzzle 1). He draws up a new design for his uncle Sol's bakery but deliberately leaves some symbols off as a good-natured test. Can you help Uncle Sol fill up the grid so that every row, column, and small square contains nine different chocolate symbols?

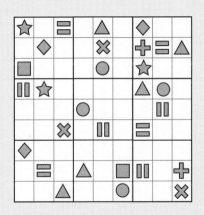

 The right-hand columns seem to offer the most possibilities.

HER FACE FITS!

Casting agent Jeremy Smythe is known for his dry sense of humor and sends out the design below—featuring various versions of the face of Dolores December, one of his best actresses—on his Happy Holidays! card toward the end of the year. The challenge is to establish the pattern of the matrix and work out which of the faces of Dolores (A–D) should fill the gap.

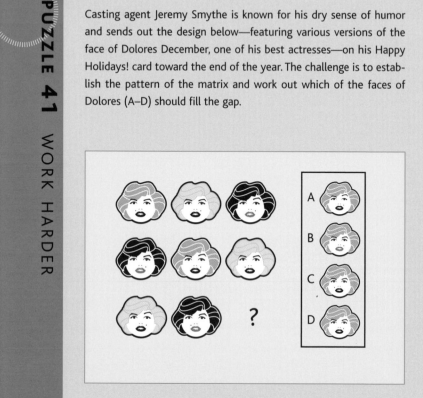

how to think TIP

Dolores December is famous for her eyebrows.

CLOCK CODE 2

Dmitry takes a risk by reusing the idea of the clock code he had agreed with Svetlana (see Puzzle 31). He tells his spy Lyudmila, "Each day for four days, the clock in the town square will be stopped at an incorrect time. Work out the sequence, and calculate what time should appear on the fifth day. If you determine that time, make contact in the usual way." Can you help Lyudmila figure out what time should appear on the fifth clock?

Returning to the square each day, Lyudmila feels she is traveling backward and forward in time.

PUZZLE 43 WORK HARDER

I HEART MATH 2

Art teacher Norton Park took the Symbol Challenge that he used with the students in his life class (see Puzzle 29) and made it the subject of a work of art. He painted it on canvas with fine oils, but also made it a working puzzle. Can you solve it?

As before, each symbol stands for a different whole number, none being less than one. In order to reach the correct total at the end of each line, what is the value of every symbol?

$$\frac{\star}{5} + \frac{\triangle}{3} = 12$$

$$\square - \star = \frac{\triangle}{9}$$

$$\frac{\square}{36} = \frac{\heartsuit}{2}$$

how to think TIP

The star must be a multiple of 5, to make a whole number in line one.

MISS PHILIPPA WALSINGHAM'S PURSE

Like her mother Lady Harriet and her brother Master Wilfred (see Puzzles 11 and 24), Miss Philippa Walsingham is difficult to please. When her father Lord Piers gives her a considerable sum to buy a new purse, Miss Philippa visits her favored local department store, Harris Halls, to browse. She handles each of the purses in turn before randomly replacing them after she makes her choice. Below are pictures of the display before and after Philippa's visit. Which does she buy?

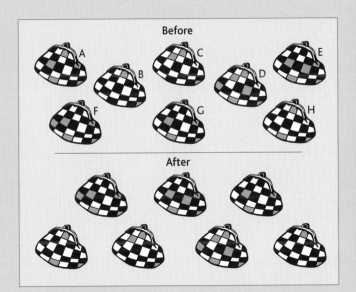

Why not photocopy the page and compete with a friend or family member to finish first?

PUZZLE 45 WORK HARDER

DRESSMAKERS' CHALLENGE 3

This is the third and by far the hardest of the challenges that Madame LeBrun devises for the young dressmakers at her academy (see Puzzles 13 and 33). The challenge is to determine which six shapes (three black and three white) can be fitted together to form the star shown here. Remember that the pieces may be rotated, but may not be flipped over.

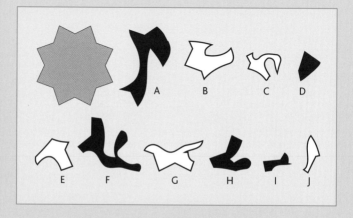

how to **think** TIP

The outer outline is angular, so the pieces will fit in a limited number of ways.

PUZZLE 46 WORK HARDER

TIME PLUS

TAKE LESS FOR EQUALITY

Designer and activist Warren creates a stylized, angular design for his campaign Take Less for Equality, which urges simple cooperative living. To promote the campaign, he devises a puzzle. Can you fill in the black squares to reveal Warren's design?

The numbers outside the grid refer to the number of consecutive black squares; each block is separated from the others by at least one white square. (So 3, 2 could refer to a row with none, one, or more white squares, then three black squares, at least one white square, two more black squares, followed by any number of white squares.)

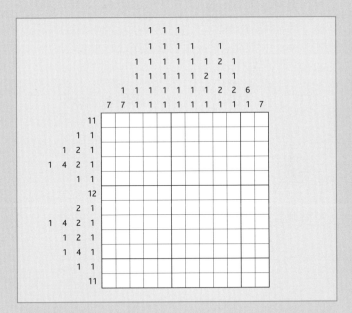

The design contains stylized versions of a minus sign ("Take less") and an equals sign (intended to symbolize "Equality").

61

PUZZLE 47 WORK HARDER

ULLA'S LETTER GRID

Ulla enjoys doing the letter grid devised by her friend and colleague Anders (see Puzzle 34) and so devises her own version to give to him. As before, the challenge is to fit the letters A, B, C, D, E, and F into the grid in such a way that each horizontal row, each vertical column, and each of the heavily outlined sections of six squares contains the six letters. Ulla fills some letters in to give Anders a start.

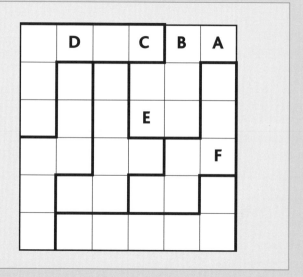

The letters in the four corner squares do not repeat.

MR. VERITY'S TANGRAMS 3

Here is a third set of the tangram challenges devised by Mr. Verity of the Upward Bounds High School art department (see Puzzles 12 and 21). He asks the students, as before, to create the shapes shown below using the seven tangram pieces provided (right). In each case you must use all of the pieces of the original tangram and they may not overlap.

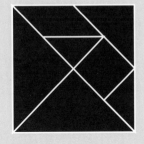

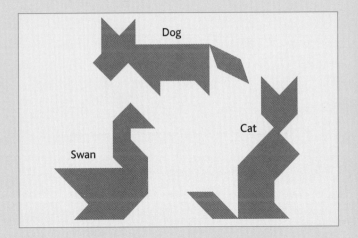

Dog

Cat

Swan

how to **think** TIP

The dog's muzzle is rather square in appearance.

HEX IN THE HOLE 2

Here's a second version of our mind-bending Hex in the Hole puzzle (see Puzzle 27). As before, the challenge is to place these seven hexagons into the central grid in such a way that where one hexagon touches another along a bold line, the contents of the adjacent triangles are the same. No rotation of any hexagon is allowed.

In the hexagon that fits bottom-left, the figure in its upper-left triangle has a value double that of the figure directly below it.

EJ'S CARPET CUBE 2

Following on from the success of the carpet cube he made for his friend Omar (see Puzzle 23), furniture designer EJ comes up with another design. He draws the design on card and gives it to his girlfriend, Sigourney, on Valentine's Day. He asks her, "When the box outline is folded to form a cube, just one of the following can be produced. Which one?"

As he'd done with Omar, EJ says to Sigourney that if she gets the answer right he will turn the design into a piece of furniture. Can you help Sigourney?

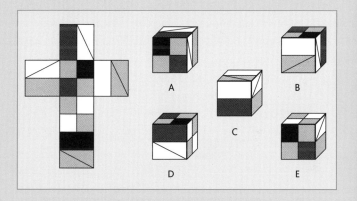

how to think TIP

It may help to turn the book around in your hands as you try to visualize the cubes.

THE
CHALLENGE

This final section gives you the chance to put the skills you have developed into practice in overcoming a series of visual and presentation challenges in an almost-real setting. You'll be called on to create visually stimulating presentations with extremely limited resources. Remember the importance of engaging the visual parts of your brain by making sketches or diagrams of any information you have to master. Consider not only what you are looking at, but also what you are looking for. It's a curious aspect of human perception that we sometimes focus so much on a foreground figure that we become oblivious to what is in the background.

DO YOU HAVE THE VISION?

Have you heard of Parkinson's Law? Devised by the British writer C. Northcote Parkinson in 1955, it declares that work expands to fill the time available. Perhaps the other side of this coin is that we often do our best work when under the pressure of deadlines. Sometimes, again, having a wealth of options and resources makes it harder to make decisions. In this thinking challenge, you're called on to provide visual input in three situations, all in a short space of time, and with severely limited resources.

The scenario is designed to provide a varied and challenging test of your ability to think visually. You'll need to be on the lookout for resources and cues to creativity, and be ready to think laterally as well as logically in order to make the most of them. Read through the text three or four times, making notes in the side columns. In thinking about the situations and requirements described, consider how in each case you could create a visual presentation that would speak simply and directly to the people you're addressing. Don't get bogged down in details—remember the big picture.

Of course there are no right or wrong answers here. The challenge is simply to come up with presentations that are creative and visually dramatic. Consider all solutions that occur to you. Some may seem unlikely, or impossible; others may seem obvious—perhaps you could give them a creative twist that would make them seem fresh.

NOTES AND CLUES

Times are hard. Two years ago you set yourself up as "Get the Picture!—Visual Thinking and Creative Services," providing design work for business planning, ideas development, trade installations, and so on. Business was great, and you built up a good client list, but the economy took a downturn and many of your clients went into administration. Now you haven't had work for three months and your commercial landlord is threatening eviction.

Nevertheless, you make sure that you keep plugging away and you are in your office every morning. And at 9 a.m. today, out of the blue, you get three offers in a matter of minutes— all of which need almost immediate attention.

First you hear from your client Amit, proprietor of Windsor Knot tie manufacturers. He has been offered a two-day occupancy of a vacant shop and needs help in designing a display before he opens at 10.30 a.m. All he has is an empty shop, a table, a few chairs, his stock

69

NOTES AND CLUES

of ties, and twelve shop mannequins—nine male, three female. You have one hour to create something.

The second offer is also from Amit. If you can help him with the shop, he says, he'll hire you to put together a presentation on his business plan for potential investors. "I want to tell the investors that with so many people losing their jobs, although the market for luxury executive ties is falling apart I'm planning to go into school and club ties. I need visual input for this." "What time would that be?" you ask. "11.30 a.m.," he replies with a sheepish grin. You need the work. You take on both jobs.

Immediately you put the phone down, it rings: It is your oldest friend, Julius, a writer/director/ actor, who at the last minute has been offered the chance to pitch his idea for a horror movie to two wealthy producers. "The only catch," he says, "and this is why I thought of you, is they say they are bored of verbal pitches. They want a purely visual pitch—no words."

NOTES AND CLUES

You agree to help. "What's the idea for the movie?" you ask. "It's Sweeney Todd for the takeout age," he says. "You know the story of Sweeney Todd, the barber who killed his enemies and clients and put them into pies? This is the story of an insane takeout pizza delivery guy who murders customers and uses them for his pizza toppings." "What time is the meeting?" you ask, fearing the worst. "12.30 p.m.," Julius replies, "is that a problem?"

Once again, you take the job on. The main difficulty is that Julius has no resources at all. So you look around your office for inspiration. There is an old takeout pizza box, with a half-eaten pizza, a knife, and your son's toybox and modeling clay.

Can you help? Can you come up with a makeshift shop design? Can you devise a visual presentation for Amit's business plan? Do you have the vision to create a visual pitch for Julius's movie? It's 9.30. You have three hours. What do you do? Or rather, how do you think?

THE
ANSWERS

Try to use this section as a source of inspiration. We all get stuck sometimes—we feel we're out of ideas and need help. If you're really stymied, by all means look up the answer to the problem. After reading the solution, try to rehearse the steps in the thinking process that led to the given answer, so you can adapt the strategy for future use, both with other puzzles in the book and in real life. As with all puzzles, it's possible that you may sometimes find an alternative solution—a sign that your visual intelligence is developing apace and you're putting it to good use.

PUZZLE 1 SUDOKU BAKE

The completed design for the sudoku cake is as shown (right). Sudoku puzzles, whether made with pencil and paper or chocolate symbols and cake, provide a stimulating challenge to your powers of logic and visualization.

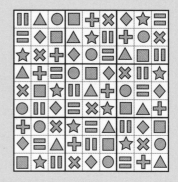

PUZZLE 2 INK SPOT MUDDLE

The stamps and prints match as follows: 1 = E, 2 = B, 3 = D, 4 = A, and 5 = C. Mr. Keitel works with images and prints all the time so his visual intelligence is well developed. He sorts out the muddle in no time, and is able to bear with his nephew's failings. However, the images are not quite what Professor Potok is looking for and he asks Mr. Keitel to try out some other designs.

PUZZLE 3 TAI'S KEYRING CHALLENGE

The keys and impressions match as follows: 1 = F, 2 = A, 3 = C, 4 = B, 5 = E, and 6 = D. We all have innate visual ability, but we need to practice in order to develop our capacity to recognize shapes and patterns.

PUZZLE 4 FUTUREWORLD

There are thirty-five blocks
missing from the original
design; the four layers of
missing blocks are as shown
(right). Challenges like this
boost your powers of
visualization, which are key
for many types of thinking.

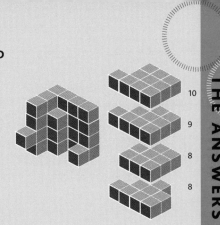

10

9

8

8

PUZZLE 5 CODE SYMBOL

The odd one out is F3, which contains a plus sign and a
question mark. It has neither a heart nor a zero (the two
symbols for line 3). You'll need a good eye for detail to
work out Sunil's code and find his odd one out.

PUZZLE 6 FORWARD AND BACK

The necessary routes, forward (bottom left) and back (bottom right),
are shown below. Puzzlers have enjoyed doing visual puzzles such as
mazes and tangrams since the era of the pharaohs in Egypt and the
kings of ancient China. In solving them, your brain works in the same
way it does when making sense of the world around you—by fitting
together perspectives and pieces until a pattern can be seen.

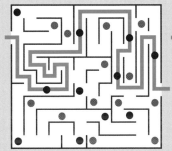
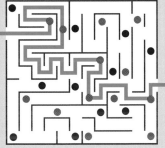

75

PUZZLE 7 DANIELLE'S DESIGNS

The matching designs are D and E. Spot-the-same puzzles like this give you practice in looking closely and seeing patterns. Brandon is really taken with Danielle's designs. He uses them in his upmarket café, The English Tea Rooms. His customers love them and soon he is stocking Danielle's designs for sale.

PUZZLE 8 COUNTRYWIDE

The differences are as follows. In scarecrow A, the crow has only one wing; in scarecrow B, some straw is missing from the left foot; in scarecrow C, the patch on the trousers is black; in scarecrow D, the cravat is black; in scarecrow E, the nose is missing. Like Danielle's Designs (Puzzle 7), this tests your eye for detail in a fun way.

PUZZLE 9 BUCKINGHAM'S BATTLESHIPS

The Battleships grid as completed by Jeremiah is as shown (right). Battleship games are good for testing and developing your ability to think clearly at speed.

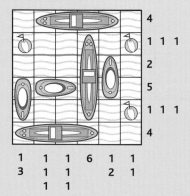

PUZZLE 10 BAZ TILES

The answer is tile A. Each column and row of the matrix contains two black stars and one black circle. Each row and column also contains two gray stars and a gray triangle. Finally, each row and column contains one image with a white star in the center, one with a white star in the top-right square, and one

with the white star in the bottom-left square. The missing image should therefore have a black star, a gray triangle, and a white star in the bottom-left corner. The completed matrix is as shown (above).

PUZZLE 11 LADY HARRIET'S HAT

Lady Harriet bought hat F. This is another test of your eye for detail and ability to see patterns. It provides further practice in looking closely. Alfredo's assistant, Maria, can see patterns quickly and rearranges the display within a minute of Lady Harriet sweeping out of the shop.

PUZZLE 12 MR. VERITY'S TANGRAMS

The shapes can be made from the pieces as shown (right). This is a version of the ancient Chinese dissection puzzle of tangrams, in which players are asked to make shapes using seven 2D shapes (tans). Like other ancient and perennially popular puzzles (such as mazes), tangrams stimulate diverse parts of the brain.

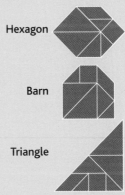

Hexagon

Barn

Triangle

PUZZLE 13 DRESSMAKERS' CHALLENGE

Parts A, E, G, and J all fit together, as shown
(right). The puzzle provides key practice for
Madame LeBrun's dressmakers in fitting parts
to a pattern. This kind of challenge develops
the potential for visual thinking.

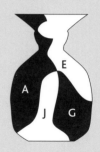

PUZZLE 14 ANCIENT TABLETS

The answer is B (as shown, right). Each large
block makes a quarter-turn clockwise every
time. This is a really stimulating thinking
challenge because it requires you to make
both close observation of the patterns and
the lateral step of considering whether the
large blocks might be rotated.

PUZZLE 15 ANGEL'S JEWELS

The goblet shape shown (right) is the only one that
appears twice in Angel's drawer. If you look back to
page 26, you can see this shape in the top left of the
picture and then, in a different orientation, on the
right side of the picture.

PUZZLE 16 ELVIS'S TIGHT FIT

The outline of the 12 Ls within the grid is as shown (right). This is quite a demanding test of pattern recognition and visual logic. If you find it difficult, don't forget that it's the difficult tests that really stimulate your thinking. Elvis based the puzzle on the game "L and O" created by his friend, philosophy teacher Ella (see Puzzle 12 in *How to Think: 50 Puzzles for Tactical Thinking*).

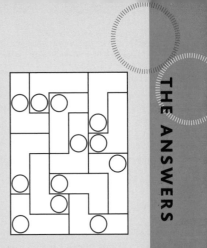

PUZZLE 17 COUNTRYWIDE 2

The matching kites are C and D. Developing your concentration and your eye for detail using simple spot-the-same puzzles like this helps you think more swiftly and effectively and makes it easier to meet everyday challenges at work, college, or home. In the game Countrywide, if the player fails to pick the right pair or is too slow, the kites float away and the field becomes a mudbath in which it is impossible for the elves to keep their footing.

PUZZLE 18 TAI'S KEYRING CHALLENGE 2

The keys match with the impressions as follows: 1 = C, 2 = D, 3 = A, 4 = F, 5 = B, and 6 = E. It's worth developing your powers of concentration and attention to detail with puzzles like this as an ability to think visually can really add drive and energy to your mental performance.

PUZZLE 19 CHANCER'S SHADOW

D is Chancer's correct shadow. In addition to honing your attention to detail, this kind of puzzle provides good practice in holding visual information in your short-term memory.

PUZZLE 20 ANCIENT TABLETS 2

The correct choice is C, as shown (right). Each letter in the top row moves back four places in the alphabet, those in the middle row move forward three places, and those in the bottom row move backward two places in the alphabet. This takes Homer's visual pattern challenge to

A	N	G
P	Q	L
J	T	P

a new level by incorporating the movement of letters. Scientists tell us that the best puzzles for training the brain are those, like this, that fire activity in several diverse brain areas.

PUZZLE 21 MR. VERITY'S TANGRAMS 2

The tangrams fit together as shown (right) to make an arrow, a rabbit, and a letter E. Mr. Verity's tangrams really energize the thinking of his art students. He finds that their visual creativity is high after solving the tangram challenges as a warm-up.

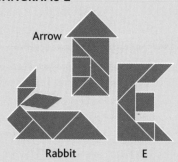

Arrow

Rabbit

E

PUZZLE 22 INK SPOT MUDDLE 2

The stamps and prints match as follows: 1 = C, 2 = D, 3 = B, 4 = E, and 5 = A. Mr. Keitel's all for promoting visual thinking. He believes that unless you have a well-developed visual intelligence, you cannot think to your full potential. He would agree with the proposal that as you progress through this book you are laying the groundwork for greatly improved thinking performance at work and in other areas of your life.

PUZZLE 23 EJ'S CARPET CUBE

The answer is D, as shown (right). Omar completes maze puzzles and thinking challenges all the time, so his visual intelligence is well primed and he gets the answer right almost at once. EJ makes the Carpet Cube for Omar. The sides and crosspieces on the carpet are reinforced, so when folded as a cube the piece is sturdy enough to use as a seat. Omar's friends all comment on the Carpet Cube, and agree that it's a "really neat piece of furniture."

PUZZLE 24 MASTER WILFRED WALSINGHAM'S

SPINNING TOP Master Wilfred purchases spinning top G. You really need to concentrate on the details of the design to solve this puzzle. It provides another good opportunity to develop your visual logic and powers of attention.

PUZZLE 25 ANGEL'S JEWELS 2

The round-edged jewel shown (right) is the only one to appear twice. Angel takes the pair of stones, places them in a padded envelope, seals it, and hands it to the courier. Some people find these visual recognition tests easy while for others they are much more difficult. How do you perform on tests like this and Puzzle 15? Angel herself is practiced at seeing and combining shapes and finds the pair swiftly.

PUZZLE 26 COUNTRYWIDE 3

The differences are as follows. In A, the top shape on the upper part of the right wing is black. In B, the right antenna is missing. In C, the lower left wing is missing its "tail." In D, a white spot is missing from the lower part of the right wing. In E, an additional black spot has appeared on the upper part of the left wing. Bennie finds them all, and the game pops up a message box saying, "Well done! Great eye for detail!" The player then has to jump up and grab a butterfly and fly off to Level 4 of Countrywide.

PUZZLE 27 HEX IN THE HOLE

The hexagons fit together as shown (right). The skill needed to hold possible alignments in your mind's eye while imagining the movement of the hexagons is one that can develop with practice. In solving this puzzle, you've developed your ability to see and plot connections at speed.

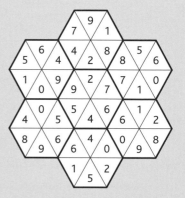

PUZZLE 28 FUTUREWORLD 2

There are thirty-four blocks missing from the original design. The five layers of missing blocks are as shown (right). In challenging you to visualize how the blocks would fit together in three dimensions, while also counting how many are missing, the puzzle forges diverse brain connections—and, as we have seen, a well-connected brain is primed to think.

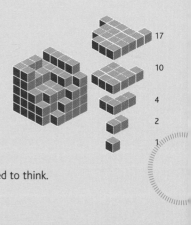

PUZZLE 29 I HEART MATH

The answers to the Symbol Challenge are as follows: Heart = 13, Square = 12, Star = 11, Triangle = 8. The first time that Norton introduced the game, the students in the life class groaned, but they soon came to see that the visual–mathematical work-out improved their thinking and vision. Whether you're at work, college, or home, try to keep challenging yourself to practice visual thinking—it will undoubtedly improve your mental performance.

PUZZLE 30 CHRISTINA'S CHOCOLATE CHALLENGE

The three lines should be drawn as shown (right) to create five sections, each containing one each of the six different chocolates. Christina's

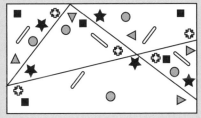

puzzle develops visual logic. Angie struggles initially, but perseveres—and suddenly sees where the lines should go.

PUZZLE 31 CLOCK CODE

The fifth clock should show 3.43 (right). The time differences on clocks 1–4 are as follows: plus 1 hour 13 minutes (clock 1 to clock 2), plus 1 hour 31 minutes (clock 2 to 3), plus 1 hour 13 minutes (clock 3 to 4). The difference between clock 4 and 5 should be plus one hour 31 minutes. If you add one hour 31 minutes to 2.12 (clock 4), you get 3.43. Svetlana works this out and sends in her report, which uncovers the identity of a double agent and saves many lives.

PUZZLE 32 CODE SYMBOL 2

The answer is C4. It contains a flower symbol, and these belong in row 3. Sunil prides himself on his concentration and well-developed visual logic, and solves the puzzle with relative ease. How did you do? Are you finding that your performance on puzzles demanding detailed inspection and visual logic is improving with practice as you work through the book?

PUZZLE 33 DRESSMAKERS' CHALLENGE 2

Piece E is not required. Pieces A, B, C, D, F, G, H, I, and J fit together to make the camel as shown (right), with D and J forming the legs. Madame LeBrun's assembly puzzles have a fearsome reputation among her students past and present. The students agree that the visual and mental logic developed by the puzzles really helps in other parts of their work.

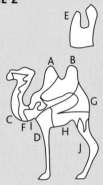

PUZZLE 34 ANDERS' LETTER GRID

The letters should be arranged in the grid as shown (right). You'll see that each horizontal row, each vertical column, and each of the heavily outlined sections of six squares contains the six letters. Ulla enjoys the challenge. "A kind of sudoku with letters," she murmurs to the friendly seagull, Silver, that is perched on her snow-covered windowsill.

A	F	B	D	C	E
F	E	C	A	B	D
B	C	D	F	E	A
E	D	A	C	F	B
C	A	E	B	D	F
D	B	F	E	A	C

PUZZLE 35 BUCKINGHAM'S BATTLESHIPS 2

One possible solution to the second Battleships grid as completed by Jeremiah is as shown (right). Captain Buckingham's grids provide a good work-out for Jeremiah's applied logic and visual intelligence. Jeremiah persuades the captain to submit them to the local

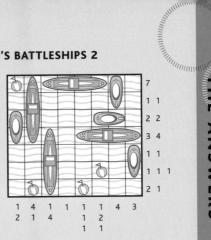

newspaper, *The Sea Gull*, and the puzzles are soon a favorite of many denizens of their small coastal town.

PUZZLE 36 ELVIS'S TIGHT FIT 2

The outline of the 12 Ls within the grid is as shown (right). As we have seen, Ella had earlier created her own version of this game (see answer to Puzzle 16), so she is practiced in recognizing and manipulating patterns; although this version is quite a challenge, she solves it in seven minutes. How did you do?

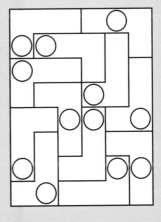

PUZZLE 37 THE SKELETON OF SØREN SØRENSEN

B is the correct shadow. A is missing the bottom ribs. C has the fingers of one hand too close together. D has thin shin bones. Christian Nygaard is the winner of Karen's competition, which generates publicity in the local newspaper and boosts visitor numbers, thus keeping her boss happy.

PUZZLE 38 FUTUREWORLD 3

There are eighty-six blocks missing from the original cube. The six layers of missing blocks are as shown (right). The puzzle provides a stern test of your number-juggling skills, as well as developing your ability to imagine the alignment of the blocks in space—don't be afraid to use pencil and paper to help

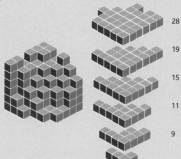

yourself keep track of the necessary mental arithmetic (remember the Notes and Scribbles pages at the back). Reaching the guru's cave is only the beginning of a new set adventures in FutureWorld; players embark on a new level as a sadhu or sadhvi (holy man or woman).

PUZZLE 39 NO WAY OUT?

The path from one dot to the other is as shown (right).

PUZZLE 40 SUDOKU BAKE 2

Uncle Sol completes the puzzle, with a bit of a struggle, as shown (right). This design is harder to complete than in Puzzle 1 because Isaac leaves more spaces blank, and it's just possible that you may find your own solution. Brain-trainers say that sudoku puzzles build neural connections.

PUZZLE 41 HER FACE FITS!

The correct answer is D. Each row and column of the matrix has one face with black hair, one brunette, and one blonde. Each row and column has two faces with dark lipstick and one with lighter lipstick. Each row and column has a face with one raised eyebrow and two without

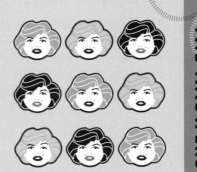

a raised eyebrow, and finally each row and column has one face with a beauty spot to the left of her mouth and two where the beauty spot is to the right. The missing image must therefore be of a brunette with dark lipstick, no raised eyebrow, and with a beauty spot to the right of her mouth. The card in fact helps Jeremy land his client a juicy role in a TV biopic of artist Andy Warhol, so she's more than happy.

PUZZLE 42 CLOCK CODE 2

The clock should show 10.55 as shown (right). Lyudmila works out that the clocks show times of plus 2 hours 10 minutes, minus 3 hours 20 minutes, and plus 4 hours 30 minutes, so the final clock should show a time of minus 5 hours 40 minutes. If you take the time on the fourth clock (4.35) and subtract 5 hours 40 minutes, you get 10.55. Lyudmila sees this time on day five and sends in her report.

PUZZLE 43 I HEART MATH 2

The answers to the Symbol Challenge painting are as follows: Heart = 1, Square = 18, Star = 15, Triangle = 27. Norton Park's painting attracted a good deal of interest and he was commissioned to make several more.

PUZZLE 44 MISS PHILIPPA WALSINGHAM'S PURSE

Miss Philippa buys purse A. Like the other Walsingham puzzles, this is a version of an odd-one-out challenge designed to provide a real test of your close attention and visual memory.

PUZZLE 45 DRESSMAKERS' CHALLENGE 3

Parts B, C, F, G, H, and I are all used, fitting together as shown (right). A, D, E, and J are not needed. Like Madame LeBrun's earlier dressmakers' puzzles, this jigsaw challenge powerfully develops alertness to visual connections, a key reason why this genre of puzzles is valued so highly at the academy. Highly intricate jigsaw puzzles of this type provide a stern test for your visual intelligence.

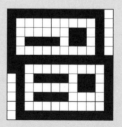

PUZZLE 46 TAKE LESS FOR EQUALITY

Warren's design is as shown (right). He has it made up on the front of T-shirts with his slogan, "Take a little less ...", while on the back of the T-shirts he has "... and leave more to go around."

PUZZLE 47 ULLA'S LETTER GRID

The completed grid should look as shown (right). Anders finds the letter grid a stimulating challenge to his verbal and visual thinking. He is puzzled, however, to find a line drawing of a seagull on the edge of the page, and when he asks Ulla, she explains that a tame seagull named Silver was watching as she devised the puzzle and she must have absent-mindedly drawn his portrait.

F	D	E	C	B	A
A	F	B	D	C	E
B	A	D	E	F	C
E	B	C	A	D	F
C	E	F	B	A	D
D	C	A	F	E	B

PUZZLE 48 MR VERITY'S TANGRAMS 3

The tangrams fit together as shown (right) to make a dog, swan, and cat. Like the three missing-blocks challenges (see Puzzles 4, 28, and 38), Mr. Verity's tangram puzzles provide a good opportunity to develop your powers of imaginative visualization.

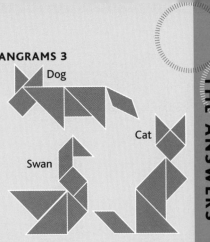

PUZZLE 49 HEX IN THE HOLE 2

The seven hexagons fit together as shown (right). The Hex in the Hole puzzles make your short-term numerical and visual memory work hard as you imaginatively plot the six possible directional movements of each hexagon, and the alignments these would produce.

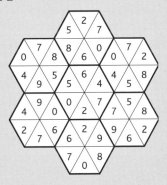

PUZZLE 50 EJ'S CARPET CUBE 2

The answer is cube B, as shown (right). For this puzzle you need to visualize how a two-dimensional design appears in three dimensions from a number of angles and this is a good challenge for your visual logic and imagination.

Sigourney finds the correct answer quickly—she works as a graphic designer and has a well-developed visual sense. The black-and-white carpet cube EJ makes for her is very chic but also sturdy. Many months later, he proposes to her while she is sitting on it.

89

THE CHALLENGE: DO YOU HAVE THE VISION?

In the shop with Amit you see that you really have nothing to work with but the mannequins, the ties, and a few pieces of furniture. One solution could be to clear the mannequins away and make an attractive display of the ties on the table and chairs. But you decide to go for a bit more visual drama.

You put ties on four male mannequins, and arrange two sitting on chairs at one end of the table, with two standing behind as if discussing business. You take one female mannequin and put a knotted tie around her head, then arrange a male mannequin beside her in such a way that she appears to be leading him by the tie he is wearing. Then you loop several ties together and arrange four mannequins in two opposed pairs, male and female: they are pulling at the ties between them as if having a tug of war, using the ties as a rope. The final two mannequins you arrange looking down at a knot of ties on the floor as if at a snakes' nest or extravagantly colored plant. When the doors open, you see quite a few passers-by stop, look, and come in. Amit is pleased. The till is soon ringing.

For Amit's meeting with the investors you take only a large pad and marker pen—materials you already have in your office. As Amit introduces his strategy you draw a simple box to represent a Factory, then three more labeled Office, School, and Club. Your draw an arrow linking Factory to Office, as he explains his original business was supplying luxury ties to executives. You then cross out the arrow as he reveals that this market is no longer active enough. As he details his plan to make ties for schools and members of sports clubs, you draw new arrows linking the Factory to the boxes marked School and Club. You suggest that executives have children at school and belong to clubs, and so may be able to recommend the business. At this point you add dotted lines from Office to the other boxes. One of the investors suggests considering making corporate uniform ties for airlines or train companies and at this point you are able to add a very simple airplane or train to the picture, with an arrow linking this to the Factory. Because you enjoy drawing, you're able to add a large striped tie down the side of the sheet; on the knot you write "Windsor Knot" and then add Schools, Clubs, and Corporate, one on each of the stripes.

That job done, you rush off to Julius's meeting with the producers. You have a few minutes in your office to make the presentation. First you take the half-eaten pizza in its box and make a human figure from the modeling clay. You then lay the figure face-down on the pizza and stick the knife in its back. You lay one of the small figurines from the toybox on the pizza and position another to look as if she is running away. This is what Julius presents to the producers: an open pizza box, with a half-eaten pizza; on top lies a human figure with a knife in its back, beside a second corpse and a fleeing victim.

You return, exhausted, to your office. Almost at once, Amit calls you to say that he has had really good takings at the shop so far and that the investors are putting money in, so he is able to pay your fee. Later, Julius calls round to say that the producers loved the presentation, are backing the film, and that he is now going ahead with production under the title *Pizza Feaster*. Would you like a cameo role? Also, he can pay your fee, so you are able to square up with your landlord.

You sit back in your chair, satisfied that a good day's work has been done. The afternoon is still young. Then the telephone rings again ...

The 21st-Century Brain: Explaining, Mending, and Manipulating the Mind by Steven Rose, Vintage 2006

The Back of the Napkin: Solving Problems and Selling Ideas with Pictures by Dan Roam, Portfolio 2008

Descartes' Error: Emotion, Reason, and the Human Brain by Antonio Domasio, Vintage 2006

Eye and Brain: The Psychology of Seeing by Richard Gregory, OUP 1997

The Intelligent Eye: Learning to Think by Looking at Art by David Perkins, Getty Education Institute for the Arts 1994

My Name is Asher Lev by Chaim Potok, Penguin 1994

The Non-designer's Design Book by Robin Williams, Peachpit Press 2008

Phantoms in the Brain: Human Nature and the Architecture of the Mind by V.S. Ramachandran and Sandra Blakeslee, Fourth Estate 1999

Presentation Zen: Simple Ideas on Presentation Design and Delivery by Garr Reynolds, New Riders 2008

Splendours and Miseries of the Brain: Love, Creativity, and the Quest for Human Happiness by Semir Zeki, Wiley/Blackwell 2008

Studio Thinking: The Real Benefits of Visual Arts Education by Lois Hetland, Ellen Winner, Shirley Veenema, and Kimberly M. Sheridan, Teachers' College Press 2007

Thinking in Pictures by Temple Grandin, Bloomsbury 2006

Visual Intelligence: How We Create What We See by D.D. Hoffman, Norton & Co 2000

Visual Thinking by Rudolf Arnheim, University of California Press 2004

"Visual Thinking" by Douglas Coupland, essay in *Granta 101*, 2008

Visual Thinking: For Design by Colin Ware, Morgan Kaufmann 2008

Websites:
www.creativityworks.net
www.designinginteractions.com
www.digitalroam.typepad.com/
digital_roam/visual_thinking

Cartoon websites for visual stimulation and a little light relief:
www.dilbert.com
www.xkcd.com

the how to think series

Puzzles to help you ...

... think
LATERALLY
to solve
problems

... think
CREATIVELY
to generate
fresh ideas

... think
LOGICALLY
to make
reasoned
decisions

... think
QUICKLY
to cope in a
crisis

... think
TACTICALLY
to work out
strategies

... think
VISUALLY
to improve
communication

The Author

Charles Phillips is the author of 20 books and a contributor to more than 25 others, including *The Reader's Digest Compendium of Puzzles & Brain Teasers* (2001). Charles has investigated Indian theories of intelligence and consciousness in *Ancient Civilizations* (2005), probed the brain's dreaming mechanism in *My Dream Journal* (2003), and examined how we perceive and respond to color in his *Colour for Life* (2004). He is also a keen collector of games and puzzles.

EDDISON SADD EDITIONS
CONCEPT Nick Eddison
EDITORIAL DIRECTOR Ian Jackson
ART DIRECTOR Elaine Partington
DESIGNER Malcolm Smythe
PRODUCTION Sarah Rooney

IMAGINE PUZZLES LTD
EDITOR Ali Moore
PUZZLE-CHECKER Sarah Barlow

PUZZLE PROVIDERS
Moran Campbell da Vinci, Puzzle Press